WHAT *Really* GOES ON IN THAT HEAD OF YOURS?

Dear Andi,

Thank you for buying my book!
You are a great friend
Lots of love

Christy Kollozor

What Really Goes On In That Head Of Yours?

CHRISTY KOLESZAR

authorHOUSE®

AuthorHouse™ UK Ltd.
1663 Liberty Drive
Bloomington, IN 47403 USA
www.authorhouse.co.uk
Phone: 0800.197.4150

© 2013 by Christy Koleszar. All rights reserved.

No part of this book may be reproduced, stored in a retrieval system, or transmitted by any means without the written permission of the author.

Published by AuthorHouse 07/01/2013

ISBN: 978-1-4817-6930-3 (sc)
ISBN: 978-1-4817-6931-0 (e)

Any people depicted in stock imagery provided by Thinkstock are models, and such images are being used for illustrative purposes only. Certain stock imagery © Thinkstock.

Because of the dynamic nature of the Internet, any web addresses or links contained in this book may have changed since publication and may no longer be valid. The views expressed in this work are solely those of the author and do not necessarily reflect the views of the publisher, and the publisher hereby disclaims any responsibility for them.

Chapter 1

The brain is a complex organ which can take you into the depths of despair or take you on a high which seems too good to be true and which oftentimes ends up being the case. How on earth does it create such a world, a world of scents, of thoughts, of feelings, and of sights which seem so real? Can they just be in your head? You don't think so at the time. You think you are invincible, immortal, have absolutely no fear or feelings. You feel you are on the best high ever in your life, but yet to others it is just a very serious route towards danger; if not stopped or kept under control, it could end in disaster. It put me on a slippery road of adventures, visions, and experiences I will never forget.

I never thought I would experience anything so extreme in my life simply by not looking after myself. No sleep, poor diet, extreme beliefs (which some people may say are just a delusion at the best of times) would build into a whirlwind psychotic episode. Yes, this is what I am here to write about: my experience during my psychotic breakdown. Words which make you cringe, symptoms which put fear and worry into those close to me—a traumatic experience which has left me numb, in shock, and increasingly curious as to what really went wrong back in September 2007.

I can only say that the symptoms have been lingering for a lot longer than when I was diagnosed/hospitalised. I just had no idea how ill I was and how ill I was going to become. I thought things were on the way up, that my life was moving towards a more positive path of dreams and beliefs coming true and becoming real. I thought I was creating a happy, blissful, peaceful, and exciting new life, a life path I had been seeking since discovering spiritualism.

Discovering spiritualism didn't happen overnight. I wasn't getting a lot of what was being said to me at first. My friend was sharing all these websites and ideas and discoveries with me, but I just wasn't getting it, wasn't understanding where she was coming from . . . at first. Then over time I was starting to see where she was going with her various thoughts and ideas. This is when I started to discover things for myself, through other sources, other websites, a very successful medium, Chris Fleming, and a television program. This got me thinking about the paranormal, exploring Buddhism and spirituality. I wanted some answers to questions which have been left unanswered for years. I was questioning a lot of things in my life (e.g., life after death). Where do we go and what happens after we take our last breath? I was a sceptic who just thought that when you die, nothing is there waiting for you, no one is waiting for you. You don't come back or get reincarnated. I thought there was no such thing as past lives or soul mates. You don't hang around as a spirit or ghost. It just ends and that is that.

Then I had a miscarriage, and over a span of a year and a half, I had three miscarriages all together. It left a huge, gaping hole in my heart and changed me forever. This is when I really wanted to get to the bottom of things. I phoned a medium, who told me that I was very aware of spirits, and she really made me start to think there must be life after death. She told me over the phone that my miscarriages occurred because it wasn't the right time for me to be a mother, that one of the babies would be coming back when the time was right. She was able to relay messages from family members who had passed on. I am not sure about the accuracy of her messages or information, but it did intrigue me. I felt there must be something in all of this. This is when I started watching haunted programs on television. I became spooked watching a paranormal television show and grew more and more curious as to what they were showing on the shows, such as seeing orbs, being touched by something, temperature changes, and so on. What is out there that we can't see? Were these the orbs or experiences people who have died and are still around?

After the first miscarriage, I felt at times that there was a presence around me, like a small child. It was as if the child I had lost was still around me, trying to bring me comfort. A friend of mind also found this to be true after her loss. After seeing this medium, I discovered that I was able to predict the future and speak with spirits. I felt that I was able to communicate with the spirit world, and 2006 I started to read up about channelling spirits, automatic writing, tarot cards, and other forms of communication with the spirit world. I learned that I was speaking with spirits and feeling their presence, that we had spirit guides who are there to guide us and assist us with our spiritual path, helping us find happiness and love each day within ourselves and with those around us.

Soon, I was speaking with spirits through automatic writing and actually moved a few spirits onto the other side, which I just seemed to be able to do without reading up about it. This was so exciting for me, a new skill. I was also able to predict the future, speak with spirits, and give readings and spiritual counselling to friends. At last I was finally able to contribute to the world, other than just do a nine to five job.

I was also discovering past lives, as my spirit guide communicated with me through automatic writing that the reason I felt so close to one of my good friends was that we had been sisters in a past life, during the Tudor and Elizabethan periods. I was amazed to be told that, as I have always had a fascination with those time periods. So much so that I even wanted a Tudor or Elizabethan wedding. This made me believe that there must be some truth in reincarnation.

I went to a spiritual meeting one night with some friends, and there we discussed aspects of the spirit world; everyone had a chance to share their experiences with the group. When I mentioned what I was able to do (e.g., move spirits to the other side), I was told that you often carry with you in this life the skills of your past lives. That is why I found so many aspects of being a medium so easy to conduct in this life, as this is what I was able to do in a past life: to move spirits on.

I also started to do mini ghost hunts with a friend around Yorkshire, such as castles and people's homes, taking pictures and using my abilities to communicate with spirits by channelling to try and get proof that there is something out there. We did get a photo of some orbs around me as I was communicating with the spirits of people who had once lived in the location we were at.

This was all becoming a big part of my life: learning how to channel spirits more, learning how to give clearer readings to friends. I was reading up about mediumship, tarot cards, and how to find a better path spiritually. I had websites to do research from, books, and podcasts that were educating me, expanding my views on the afterlife and what is out there that we cannot see. I was meditating almost every day, using affirmations to combat any negative energy and negative thoughts. I had turned my bedroom into a lovely haven, filling it with plants, gemstones, crystals, candles, and incense. I was enjoying this new lifestyle.

A friend of mine and I had also been discussing aliens. Oh, how I had become more open to the idea of spirits being around us, but aliens? This also took me awhile to absorb and understand as being possible. I knew there were aliens out there, that UFOs and alien abductions had to be real, but to what degree was still up for debate in my eyes. I did see Paladeans in 2011 from the house I lived in. They were in the houses across the street, a neighbour's house.

I was also receiving spiritual consultations from a psychic. He steered me on the right path by saying I should follow the areas I am drawn to, and he gave me the tools to find happiness and stop repeating history in my relationships. It was getting better and better, and I felt such intense energy after my consultations. Then

I spoke to a clairvoyant, well, three to be exact, and they all told me that someone I had spoken to was my soul mate and that we would be together and work together. It was all fitting into place; I felt this man's energy and was starting to fall for him; something was there. It was all building and becoming an exciting time for me.

Was I going overboard with all of this? Is this what caused my brain to shut down and head for a breakdown? By July 2007, I was feeling on top of the world; I was falling in love and had high hopes of meeting my twin flame. I felt perhaps he would come over to the UK in September and October 2007 on business, and we would finally meet and hopefully something serious would develop. I had channelled several messages from spirits and entities which mentioned him and said that I should pursue him and keep in touch.

I started to build this world around me that included this twin flame. I was going to be working with him in the future, and we were going to be a couple.

It was around August when things really started to go downhill. I started to believe that I was talking to my twin flame telepathically. I was sitting on the bed and thought that he was tuning into me after I had been a bit upset about things in my life. I started talking and thought he was responding in my head, asking me what was wrong. I would meditate and feel that he was meditating with me and using his abilities to tap into me and actually manipulating me physically by making me walk, stopping me from moving, lowering my body during meditation. I felt we were getting closer all the time. My emotions were all over the place and had been for a very long time. I would sob uncontrollably and thought he was tapping into this and trying to comfort me. My world became worse as we explored the paranormal together telepathically and were bonding. It was a world where we were discussing how we were falling in love with each other and our meeting was meant to be. We were soul mates, twin flames, and the sooner we met face to face, the better.

By this time, because of the telepathic connection, I wasn't eating, sleeping, or looking after myself; I was up all hours. Since March, I had been sleeping with the lights on, because I was scared of the spirits and entities that were around me and visiting me in the dark and the middle of the night. For months I was becoming increasingly agitated about sleeping with the lights off, and by August, I couldn't sleep in the dark. With my emotions like a roller coaster, no sleep, and hardly eating, my mood was becoming more manic and erratic. I was pulling away from my housemates and spending more and more time in my room. I was on my laptop most nights, trying to build my blogs and speaking to friends, trying to give them spiritual counselling. My entire day was speaking telepathically to my twin flame, working till late on my laptop, and trying to arrange for him to visit me. Then one night, I started writing and was getting flight details for September. He was coming to visit me. Wow, he was able to get me to do automatic writing to relay a message to me. How was I going to tell people what was going on? I was telling people at work and in the house that we were communicating by email. It was finally going to happen. I believed it was really happening! Looking back, this is when things started to get really bad.

I was talking and laughing to myself at work, believing I was still speaking telepathically to my twin flame. I went on holiday with my parents to North Yorkshire, and in the holiday cottage, I was still disappearing to my room, so I could spend time speaking to my twin flame. It just grew from there, bonding, feeling like I was getting closer to this guy.

I started discussing with this man that I possibly had an alien in my stomach or uterus; that is where things really went downhill, and my friend said at that point she knew something was wrong with me mentally. I actually spent an entire night in my bedroom, supposedly ridding this alien from my stomach with the help of my spirit guides and the spirit world. I felt traumatised, because it hurt a lot. My uterus was being wrenched and pulled. It felt like something was being pulled from my uterus. The next morning, I told my friend what had happened to me during the night. Again

I felt this was really happening, to such an extent that when I went into work, I had to leave early and said that I was poorly.

This is when things became an unbearable roller coaster of events, all involving my twin flame.

Chapter 2

One evening in August, I was lying on the bed, supposedly speaking telepathically to my twin flame, when I thought I began to suffer from pregnancy symptoms. I put my hand on my stomach and thought I could feel a heartbeat. Then I seemed to feel this incredible energy which overwhelmed me. It was Jesus coming through, saying that I was carrying my twin flame's child through immaculate conception due to true love felt between us as twin flames. We felt such intense emotion for each other that through astral travel, my twin flame and I had conceived a child. The spirit told us that my twin flame had been Joseph in a past life and I had been Mary, and this child would be the messiah. Then that changed and the spirit said that my twin flame and I together would be the messiah but that this child would have incredible abilities.

My twin flame and I were told by the spirit of my grandmother that in the spirit world, she had been the messiah, but now she had moved up to a higher being. She also said that people would be astral travelling into my body to feel the baby and the love between my twin flame and me so they could see how incredible this sort of love is and seek to find it within themselves. She said that I would change their thoughts and feelings about life, helping them to become more positive and live through their higher self and their heart and find happiness, love, and peace in their lives. This would lead to a chain reaction, and millions of people would start to live through the heart and influence the world to bring world peace.

In September I had resigned from my job at the same time as my twin flame had arrived in Yorkshire and was arranging to meet me. We were still communicating telepathically. This was it, we were going to meet. However, this is the start of my breakdown; my behaviour became more erratic and upsetting to others in the houseshare. One morning, my twin flame told me his sister had called; his dad was poorly and on his last legs. I then received a message from an angel that his dad was dying. Then I was told by this spirit that his dad was in his last moments of life. Soon after, it appeared that his dad had passed away and was visiting me in spirit before he passed on to the spirit world. I thought that I had spoken to his guardian angel (who is there to meet him and move him on), telling me that they were so grateful that I was helping him and my twin flame to bond so he can find closure and forgiveness before he passed on. His dad then spoke to my twin flame, saying he would be leaving his inheritance, which meant we would be able to go on holiday and my twin flame and I would definitely be married one day. Therefore, I would be financially secure forever and never have to work again. This meant that I would be supported and it was fine that I had resigned from my job. It was my twin flame's intent to support me financially so I could focus on my career as a medium.

I arranged to meet my twin flame in York. We believed that as soul mates, we would be meeting on the river in York as we once did in a past life. So I packed my bag, brought along chocolates and photos of me, and headed out the door, telling my housemates I was going to meet this guy for real. I headed on the train, speaking telepathically to him along the way. We were both excited about finally meeting and agreed that it would be fantastic. I was so nervous and couldn't believe I was going to be meeting him face to face. I got off the train and walked past the Royal York Hotel, down to the river. He was staying at the Royal York but wanted to meet at the river, where we had first met in our past life. It was going to be explosive and emotional.

I sat on the river and waited for him to turn up. He told me to close my eyes and feel his energy. Then things went downhill again, as he kept saying he feels I don't trust him, that if I don't trust him and give him the feeling that I am calm and confident in us being together, that he can't meet me, that the energies will be too strong, and he doesn't want our first meeting to be disastrous. So he kept asking me to sense where he was, that I had to be calm and have no fear of meeting him. This continued and eventually he told me to start walking. He manipulated my legs so I walked away from the river, and eventually I ended up at the hotel where he was supposedly staying.

I sat in reception talking to him telepathically, and he said that because of the combination of his father dying, his mood, and the energy he was getting from me, he wasn't sure if we should meet. He didn't want to see anyone from the public, as he was depressed about losing his father. The combination was wrong, and he felt we would end up arguing, and he didn't want our first meeting to be a disaster.

I had now been in York for three hours and still had not met up with him. I asked him which room he was in and said I would come to him. I climbed the stairs, and he told me to sense his energy and come to the second floor. I went to the second floor and told him to just come out of his room so we could meet. He said I was too angry now from wasting all this time and that our moods would clash and we would fight. He also said he wasn't sure if I was right for him, that he was having second thoughts about us. I eventually knocked on the door of the room I thought he was in but no one answered.

Eventually I said, "I have had enough of this situation and I am going home." Every time I said this and tried to walk away, he manipulated my legs to walk back to him in the hotel. By this time, people in the hotel were looking at me, wondering why I was hanging around. I left the hotel and said I was going home. He said to me he would come out, and as I got to the car park, he said, "Go to the station and I will meet you there."

I walked to the train station and waited again for ages. I then said I would walk back to the hotel. When I arrived at the hotel, I thought I could see him. A black car passed me and I thought I saw him inside the car. The car came out of the car park of the hotel, and I thought I saw him driving. He said that was his car and that he was wearing that coloured shirt. I told him to come back to the hotel; by this time it had been nearly four hours since I first arrived. He said he was stuck in traffic and to stay there, he would be back. I walked out to the station to try and find his car in the traffic jam. I burst into tears when I thought I had seen him. I fell apart, sobbing uncontrollably that I had seen him briefly and now he was gone again.

After another hour, I said I was cold and tired and people were looking at me. I couldn't wait anymore and I wanted to go home. He kept getting angry, saying how he hated traffic jams and he was lost but would be back soon. In the end, I left and got back on the train and went home. Then we discussed him coming to Leeds to meet me, and this is when things got even more interesting. My housemates were wondering where he was and why he kept letting me down. I believed he wanted to meet me and was just as upset as me that we still hadn't met. According to him, it was a combination of me not trusting him and still being too scared. The energies had to be right, as we were twin flames, and if the energies were unbalanced, it would be a disastrous reunion.

There were other days like this in Leeds, where I waited for my twin flame and he didn't show because he said the same thing: that I didn't trust him enough and the energy was not right. Day after day for that week, I sat on a wall, on the front steps, on a street corner waiting for the man of my dreams to arrive, but in reality, he was never in Yorkshire to begin with. This was something my brain had created. This was the world I was living in. There were days when I waited for hours on a street corner, being told to feel his energy.

I was supposed to follow his energy and try to find where he was. Of course, in reality, this is impossible. Can you find someone this way? In my world, this was the challenge being put to me. Of course I never found him and wandered from street to street and back to the house, cold, angry, and upset.

Chapter 3

The next scenario that started to take place was that people were astral travelling into my body and around me; evil spirits were trying to stop my twin flame and I from meeting. I also had to deal with moving through different dimensions; my twin flame kept changing dimensions and couldn't get to me.

People do astral travel in real life, but in my world, everyone could do it. I was also talking to my friends and family telepathically. It was a combination of my twin flame and I trying to meet and combating evil spirits in the house and around me. It was good versus evil the entire time these scenes were taking place. One time, my twin flame was in Leeds, down the road from where I lived, but he was not able to walk to my house or to me. He was stuck on a street corner near me, overtaken by evil spirits and unable to walk to me.

One night, my friend's brother and my twin flame travelled to the other side to try and hunt down a bad angel and kill her to end her evil influence. My mother was also with me (astrally), and we were walking near our home, trying to find where my twin flame had parked his car. I had gotten dressed up to meet him, but again he was unable to meet me. This time, it was because we were in the wrong dimension. We were dealing with changing different dimensions; at first it was only my twin flame who could change dimensions. He kept trying to get to my house, but he parked the car on one dimension and was wandering around trying to find his car, which wasn't where he left it because he had changed dimensions. How did he do this? It seemed to be through a hypnotic state; he would close his eyes for a moment and was taken to the next level instantly by being in a certain state of consciousness. In my world, this was possible. The other problem that developed was that my twin flame suffered from agoraphobia; he was having trouble finding the courage to come and see me.

The entire time this was taking place, I was alone but talking telepathically to my parents and to him. Slowly, other people like my brothers and friends of my twin flame were joining the conversations telepathically and through astral travel. This was becoming increasingly stressful for me, because I had voices in my head which would speak to me. I tried to respond out loud and in my head the entire time. Trying to speak in your head is not easy. It is very trying to think the words in your head and get a response back as words in your head. I was on my own for most of this time.

This is how I spent my days, and the whole time, I felt like there were all these people around me in spirit through astral travel who could see me, but I couldn't see them.

Chapter 4

One morning, I was told by the spirit world that I had to relay a message to the world telepathically, saying that I was the messiah and I would heal the world; spirits told me that people would die and then be resurrected by my powers and healing abilities. This was one of the worst moments for me, for chaos ensued and people were not coming back from dying in their sleep. I had to keep talking to them telepathically and bring them round, to tell them that they wanted to live and to open their eyes and come back. Eventually they did, but I was told that there were people who just didn't want to come back and wouldn't. Millions would be dead in their beds, and this was nature's way of sifting out the negative people from the world.

I was also supposed to visualise a protective shield around the earth to prevent an asteroid from colliding with it. I succeeded in stopping the asteroid and bringing people back from the dead. However, the chaos continued as people still didn't want to come back; I had to keep repeating over and over, "Open your eyes and wake up," "Open your eyes and wake up." Eventually, everyone came back. This kept happening; the energy would get too negative and people would die again, and I had to change the energy to positive and bring them back. Death was everywhere, but eventually everyone woke up. It was my task to convince people to change their attitude to be more positive and create positive energy around them, to get rid of as much negativity in the world as possible.

Chapter 5

There was speculation that there was a cult in my house; this wasn't the case in real life, but in my world, this was believed.

There was a day when everyone in the house had died, and no one was coming back. I couldn't bring them back, and I had to experience the smell and the sense of these dead bodies in the house; I needed to help a family member who had been through a war and had seen dead bodies. You see, it was all linked, like a chain. Those linked with me had to go through things too, to relive their past to heal so we could all heal and thus create a domino effect. It was felt that the cult experience had to be relived so this family member could heal. This was horrific for me, as it sure felt real—too damn real. As it happened, there was silence in the house; I listened and then the smell came, the smell of dead bodies. My housemates had all died, and they weren't coming back. I could smell the rotting bodies; it was horrific.

Some people involved in astral travel told me that there was too much negativity around, that people all over the world were dead; bodies were lying in the street because they didn't want to come back. These people had been too negative, including my housemates.

I was told not to go into the rooms, to stay in my room. Then I was told that everyone was going to have to change dimensions, as my twin flame and I had to meet and we had to be away from the negativity. I was told that if we met, there would be world peace and more positive energy in the world. So, I had to go outside and try and meet my twin. Also, the alien they tried to get rid of was still in me, and now the government were after me. I had to go, get the cat, and get out of the house. However, we had to do it in a way that the men in black, who could astral travel and do telepathy, couldn't pick up where I was. I was not to look at any street signs or names on buildings. If I did this too much, they would find out where I was. We had to go into hiding. A car was going to pick me up, but I had to keep my head down the whole time and not look at the car or the driver. I was to get into the back of the car and sit silently with my eyes glued to the floor the whole time. I was going to be taken to a house where my twin flame was, and once I got to the house, we would be together and safe. I had to go into hiding with him for two months until things died down.

I was told to leave the house; I went downstairs with the cat, and one of my housemates came down. He looked as if someone had died. Then I heard footsteps, and I was told that they were getting rid of the bodies (someone was speaking to me telepathically, but I had no idea who they were). I wouldn't have to worry once I got outside, because they would block out the horrible visions so I wouldn't have to be traumatised by them. I went outside, but then I was told that I was bleeding and if the men in black saw blood, they would know. They were not sure at this point if I was carrying an alien. I had to go back to the house. Then my grandmother came through in spirit and said that because we were the messiah, no harm could come to us, that we would find a route to the house where my twin flame was and be reunited. No one could harm us because I am the messiah.

I went back to the house with the cat screaming its head off. This was another giveaway! However, I was now being told they were trying to make me invisible, but any sound would make me visible again. The cat was ruining things! When I went back to the house, I was told I had to stay outside, as the government was in the house, gassing us. I could feel it while I was inside; I was feeling sick and lethargic. They were definitely gassing the house. I had to get out.

When I got outside, I was told they had left and the house was safe, that what was happening, wasn't. I was confused but surprisingly not scared. This is the thing: the entire time these events were taking place, I had no fear. I was reacting but not feeling any fear.

Back inside, I had to go back upstairs; my twin flame would astral travel, and we would have to change dimensions to get away from this all. We would go to ascension, and the sooner we got there, the better.

So I went upstairs, and I remember lying there in bed, waiting for my twin flame and I to be taken to another dimension. During this time, I was seeing all sort of things. I saw spiders that weren't real, and I saw what looked like a mini television with cartoons playing on it. I was told that this was time travel, that I was looking into the future. I saw colours and visions that were floating round me, like mini orbs coming at me, floating around the room. I saw flashes of lights all around me and was told they were fairies and angels trying to protect me. At one point, I was told to stand against the wall, where there was an energy field; if I stood in it with my twin flame astral travelling into my body, we would get energy and be protected. I could see it as well, like waves of matter, like an energy field all along the wall. When I stood against the wall, there was this incredible thrust of energy throughout my body. It was like a charge of energy that bolted throughout my body.

I remembering trying to eat; at this point, I hadn't eaten properly for days, and I was being told that I was pregnant and must eat. I don't know what day this happened, but I remember trying to cook some rice and leaving it on the stove and going back upstairs. Then smoke started billowing out around the house, and I began banging on people's doors, telling them there was a fire. My housemates came out of their rooms and were all wondering what was going on; they were very disoriented. It was the rice; it was three o'clock in the morning. I went back to my room, and all through the night, I continued to astral travel and try to heal people. People were dying and didn't want to come back, and my twin flame and I were trying to bring people back. It was horrendous. I remember that at some point, my dad was having a heart attack and dying, and my twin flame was trying to bring him back from the dead by going to the other side himself and tell him he must not let go. My twin flame brought him back; that was all taking place in my room through astral travel.

I don't remember how loud I was or what time it was by this point. It was all just an ongoing roller coaster of events that made me oblivious to the outside world. This world had sucked me in full throttle, and it was a ride I really didn't want to endure, but I had no choice. I don't remember when I ate, when I slept, or if I even had a shower most days by this point. It was building by the day, and I had people to save and had to keep working towards reuniting with my twin. That was all I was thinking. I don't even know what day it was. I do believe it was in September, the week that I was off sick, but nothing more. Looking back, I really was out of it.

I was in the city of Leeds; one day, I came home (it was Friday, the day before I went into hospital), and I don't remember how I got there or if I went to sleep.

Chapter 6

As part of bringing peace to the world and reuniting with my twin flame, I had to clear all the baggage in my life. That meant dealing with my past, my childhood, and all relationships that were left with negativity. I had to relive everything, and the only way this could be achieved was by facing everyone and dealing with everything negative in my life. This could be achieved through astral travel by facing each person, speaking to them, and then forgiving them and letting go. This would also help those in spirit to forgive me and others and move them on to the other side.

One day, when I was supposed to help move spirits on who had been in my life, it was all horrendous; I thought at the time it was real. It was spirits who had been abused and couldn't move on, and they were involved in my life (e.g., the babies I miscarried and children who has passed away but in fact hadn't). I was being told that people from my past had committed suicide, and I was the only one who could help them. I moved on maybe fifteen or twenty spirits, and they were asking me for forgiveness, or I was having to tell them to forgive themselves so they could find peace and move on. This was so draining for me, and I am sure it added to the exhaustion I was starting to experience.

There was a lot surrounding moving spirits on, and I am amazed at how I was able to do this.

Chapter 7

The day before I went into hospital, I was trying to deal with the situation with the house and the alien/government situation. I had an alien inside me as well as being pregnant, and the government were after me. I was convinced that I had brought everyone in the house back from being dead. I also thought they had been brainwashed or hypnotised by one housemate, and I couldn't look them in the eye or I might get dragged down. We had changed dimensions, but some people in the house had gone through it before me. If we were not on the same dimension, it was because it was not safe for me to do so. I kept changing dimensions to be kept safe with my twin flame. So I was by this time completely cut off from the rest of the house and the rest of the world. I was keeping my distance to avoid being hypnotised. The house felt very, very negative, and I felt drained. I believed that there were evil entities in the basement, and they were influencing the house. The housemates were doomed. There was a lot of talk telepathically of people wanting to commit suicide to get away from this dimension which was being overrun with evil. The government were slowly taking people and getting them to mass suicide.

Friday night, I had gone into town to meet up with my twin flame, and all I remember was again trying keep one step ahead of the aliens and the government. I ended up in a restaurant, but I was being followed by aliens, and they were slowly trying to take me over. I even ordered a meal but just sat there being told telepathically by my twin flame that they were all around me and slowly trying to take over my body. I had to get out of there and run away. I ended up going home (I don't remember how I got there though).

I can't recollect a lot of what happened those twenty-four hours. I don't remember sleeping, eating, and so on. All I remember is leaving the house to meet my twin flame and coming back to the house again, as he couldn't get to me. Then my twin flame told me he was in hospital, dying of cancer; I had to go back to the house, pretend I wasn't well, and ask them to drive me to the hospital so I could see him and heal him face to face. I remember going back to the house and sobbing, saying I wasn't well and I needed someone to take me to the hospital. I guess they just thought I was not well mentally and just ignored me.

The next day, Saturday, I was found by the police and taken to hospital; my housemates had said they would take me to the hospital, but I felt as if they were going to take me there for a mass suicide, so I had to decide if it was safe or not. My twin flame and I were not sure if they were taking me somewhere safe to hide or to be given an injection at hospital to die. We felt it was safe, as my good friend was with us. Then my twin flame said he was at a hotel and safe and for them to drop me off at the hotel. My housemate said we would go to the hospital first; I thought she meant we would then go to the hotel. We and the rest of the housemates got into a cab. I felt something was wrong and they all seem very hypnotised.

When we got into town and got out of the cab, I knew after wandering inside the hospital that they were not there to keep me safe; it was death for us all by lethal injection. So when we left the hospital, I fled. My housemates ran after me, and boy, was it a struggle. He nearly caught up with me, but my twin flame and all the friends who were speaking to me telepathically said run like hell and get out of there. Time was running out, and my twin flame and

I had to get together astrally, as things were getting too negative and if we didn't reunite, either face to face or astrally, the world would be doomed. I managed to lose the housemates and just wandered around; I was being followed by the aliens again. I had to find my twin flame, so telepathically my friends and my twin flame tried to help guide me to the hotel he was in; we were running out of time. I kept looking at street signs and at buildings, and whoever was after me knew where I was; I was giving away where I was by reading the street signs and was going to be caught by the government and aliens.

Now all my twin flame and I could do was meet astrally. So I laid on the grass in a park, and my twin flame astral travelled into my body. By him astral travelling into my body, the energies went back to positive. It seemed every time we reunited, the energies changed, and all was safe and well again. All that day, I wandered round Leeds, trying to keep one step ahead of the government and aliens and trying to get to where my twin flame was. Time was not on our side, because if I didn't meet with him soon, I would die. As Mary, I needed to be with my twin face to face, or the energies would become too negative and kill me. I was once again Mary and my twin flame Joseph.

I wandered around Leeds and finally got to the hotel where my twin flame was. He was going to come down and meet me. Then things went downhill again as we kept changing dimensions, and although I was in the right hotel, I was in the wrong dimension. I felt like I was dying. I left the hotel and was wandering around town. I could smell this foul scent like a rotting corpse; that was my body dying. Various friends tried to keep me going by astral travelling into my body, but the smell was too bad for them and they couldn't stay in my body.

I had to meet my twin now. I remember one spirit saying to me that if I hurried up, they would help me to reincarnate and would give me more time to meet my twin flame. I kept making wishes for another day, and extra time was given to me. I kept going into the hotel and even asked if my twin flame was in the hotel, but the staff were not happy that I was there. I think they could see I was not right in the head. Then things went downhill again, and I was dying and just had to find somewhere to go and let my body give up. I told the staff at one point to call an ambulance, that I was dying, but they just ignored me and eventually asked me to leave or they would call security. I just kept wandering, lost, in and out of the hotel. I felt disoriented, as if my legs were moving but my mind was not there. I hadn't met my twin flame, and time again was not on my side. So I went to a chair and sat down. I was dying.

A friend of mine in spirit came and helped me to reincarnate. I just let go and then came to and was alive again. Of course, nothing had really happened; I was just sitting in a chair with my eyes closed. I felt I had gone but my body came back, and I was safe again. I was on a different dimension to everyone now; I had moved up closer to ascension, leaving everyone else to catch up. I was constantly ruining things telepathically, as I couldn't do it in my head, only by talking out loud, which meant I kept giving the game away, as the aliens could hear what I was saying. Then I discovered that this technique was the way forward, as the aliens could only hear it in my mind, and if I spoke, they couldn't understand me. So we discovered that I was doing it right; I was demonstrating the safer way to speak telepathically. This technique was preventing the aliens and government from catching up with us.

I spent the rest of the evening walking around town, trying to get to my twin flame, as that is what this scenario was all about from beginning to end: us reuniting. I was not able to get to him, and we all agreed at one stage that my end was near; my parents were there telepathically, saying go to the hospital, to not die in the open. I went to a park to lie down, but my twin flame and I felt I had to keep going. I just wandered around Leeds all day and all evening. I kept going from feeling that I was dying and should just find somewhere to die to wandering around aimlessly.

The next step, after I was told that I was okay, was that everyone needed to help get me and my twin flame to ascension. I then walked to the closest hotel to check in, and that is when I felt I was being watched by the men in black. I went to the first hotel and asked if they had any rooms, and they said no. The hotel staff wore black suits, and I thought they were the government and knew who I was. I moved on to the next hotel and again asked if they had any rooms; they said no too. I felt they said no because of who I was and were watching me and closing in.

This is when it was time for me to die; I just felt it was time to go to ascension and a few friends would astrally lead me to a place where I could die and my twin flame would come with me. By dying where he was, our spirit guides and angels would help us get there. I was not scared; I just seemed to keep going. I was on a mission to find a place where the men in black couldn't find me and where I could lay down and die.

I was told to throw away my handbag, as when I came back from death, I would be a new person, with a new identity, and we had to get rid of my current identity. I threw my bag into a bush and carried on up the road, being led by my friends telepathically and astrally. We found a spot where I could lay down, and then I was told that I had been spotted and the men in black knew where I was. So several times I had to get up and move on to somewhere else. These locations were not nice: dark alley ways or behind a building in the dark. I kept going, trying to keep one step ahead, and I remember seeing some very strange things along the way. I saw what seemed to be long black vertical strips like a grid, in random spots. I don't know what they were, but I thought they were energy points. I was told later by people telepathically that if I stood in these grids, they would give me protection from those after me. I was also told that I was made invisible and no one could see me. Then I found a perfect spot, behind a nightclub next to a wall. I laid down and began the ascension process. I truly felt like my body was dying. My legs from the feet up started to go hard and numb. I lay there and various spirits assisted me; that is how it would happen. They would make my body die, and I would ascend to the next level.

The only problem was people kept coming up to me. People were coming up to me, giving me change and asking if I was okay; it was not good that they could see me. I was told by spirits that I was not to make any noise and lay absolutely still and then I would be invisible, but somehow it didn't work. At one point while I was lying there, a vortex of wind surrounded me; leaves were flying all around me, round and round. I thought it was the dark side trying to interfere, that this was a battle between me getting to ascension and them stopping me from getting there.

My ascension never took place; people kept coming up to me and interrupting the process. So I got up and went on with the evening, trying to stay hidden from the men in black. I was told to follow certain people who could help me get somewhere safe. I was told to follow one man who would lead me to a safe place. I had a sane moment and started to realise that he was probably wondering why I was following him, and so I turned and went another way. I headed back to the first hotel, and this is when things took a turn for the worst. I remember wandering around outside the hotel, thinking I had to find my twin flame. I then started to think I needed to get to a hospital.

Instead, I just wandered aimlessly around the city, feeling totally disoriented; my twin flame was telling me to get back to the hotel. I went up and down the city, trying to find a hospital but not knowing where I was going. I ended up back outside the first hotel and thought I would give up, that I was going to let myself die. I couldn't continue this way. My twin flame was furious with me, because if I died, I would throw away everything. If I kept going and we met, we would be able to save the world, but I couldn't do it. I had no more energy; I was completely disoriented by this point. I remember feeling as though I was walking, but my mind and body were numb, and I was incoherent. I just wandered around for hours.

Then my twin flame told me I had ruined everything. Everyone was depending on me, and I had thrown everything away, ruining his life and our chances. He wanted nothing more to do with me and told me not to come back to the hotel. I just felt lost and didn't know what to do. I couldn't lose him; I had to pull myself together. I remember wandering down to a square and trying to heal myself. I put my hands on my head and said that I would heal myself physically, that mentally I was stable and healed. As I said this, I seemed to get better; I wasn't as disoriented or feeling like my body was giving up on me. Then my twin flame said to come back to the hotel, he couldn't live without me and the thought of losing me was too much to bear. I headed from the square across the street to the hotel, and he told me to wait outside.

There had been a lot going on with my twin flame while he was in the hotel. He told me that the men in black had broken into his hotel room and tried to poison him, then they left. When my twin flame didn't die, they came back and tried to strangle him. As this was happening, I could sense that I was feeling whatever was happening to him, just like whatever was happening to me, my twin flame could feel. We were that connected! Every time he was dying, I brought him back with my healing energy. I brought him round from unconsciousness, from being poisoned, and from cancer. It was if we were destined as soul mates and only I could help him.

When my twin flame was okay, he said he was going to astral travel into my body so we could be closer. He told me to lie on the ground and he would astral travel into my body. When I did this, things got really interesting. He said he had a surprise for me, and it had to do with a marriage proposal. That was a complete switch from earlier in the day. He said he had been planning it, and that was why he was so angry with me. He was going to have all sorts of celebrities show up at the hotel, and he was going to propose.

This was when I was interrupted by a girl I thought was from a pop band, and when I got up, I was surrounded by people asking if I was okay. They all seemed to be celebrities; my surprise was just beginning. I felt myself saying I was so at ease with celebrities, being famous would be just perfect for me. Then I was told by my twin flame that I was a celebrity and that was why they were here. Then an ambulance showed up, and I kept saying to the people I had to go into the hotel because my boyfriend was there and he needed me to meet him so he could go back into my body. You can imagine what was going through these peoples minds: "Nutter!"

As I got into the ambulance, I kept thinking these were all actors, the paramedics were actors from a television program (*Casualty*). I was laughing at how they were trying to take my details and act like real paramedics. They were good actors, but I wasn't taking them seriously. Then the police arrived, and I thought they were the actors from another television program (*The Bill*). With all these actors around, I got so excited.

Eventually the police took my details, asked me what my address was, and then asked me to go with them. The whole time in the police car, I kept telling them I was ill and needed to go to hospital. I wasn't mentally ill, it was that I was pregnant and needed to get an injection for being Rh negative; I said that I would need a blood transfusion if they didn't hurry. It was a strange experience, because they weren't really responding, so I thought we were on different dimensions and they could only talk to me telepathically, but even that was difficult as they could hear but couldn't talk to me.

When we arrived at our destination, I thought it was the film set for the television program *Holby City*. When I was escorted in, there were two police officers. Then a member of staff there took me into a room. I kept saying I had to go to the bathroom, as all these people had astral travelled into my body and I couldn't get them out; they were stuck, including my brother. I needed to get them out, as it was draining me, and then I realised I still had an alien in my stomach and I needed to get it out. The staff let me go to the bathroom but wouldn't let me shut the door, and I was getting increasingly agitated, as I needed privacy. So in the end, I just helped get the people out astrally and tried to get the alien out, but it was stuck.

The staff took me into a room and questioned me. I kept thinking they were the government and they had tricked me into coming there, as they knew I had an alien inside me and wanted to keep me there; I was a threat. I kept speaking to them via my twin flame, saying that he was trying to relay a message to them, that he was my partner and they must let me go. So I was sitting there saying I was two people. That must have looked really bad. My friends were there astrally and they were helping me with what to say to them. My friends said they would help me escape through astral travel, so I wouldn't be in there that long.

In the end, the staff said I was being sectioned under the Mental Health Act and I was going to be staying put. I yelled that my partner was saying telepathically that he was going to sue them if they didn't let me go, that I was fine and didn't need to be there. No chance, I was stuck there. They showed me to my room, but I was determined to get out, if not by the front door then by escaping through one of the windows. I wandered round the hospital, trying to find a way out. My friends were there astrally, helping me find a way out. There wasn't one; I was doomed.

All I can remember of that twenty-four hours is that the hospital smelt of death. I spent the first bit of my time there trying to find a way to escape with the help of my friends astrally. Then I remember my parents turning up and me being told telepathically by my twin flame that we could still go to ascension and that everyone was going to commit suicide and go with us, that it wasn't safe or suitable to stay on this dimension. I remember sitting in a room with my parents, thinking that we were going to sit around a table and die there and then, that some of them were going to take cyanide and just go in their sleep. I remember just going into my room and saying that I had to reunite with my twin flame and I wanted to do it alone. So I got into bed and closed my eyes, ready for the spirits to take me and my twin flame to the next dimension. I was told that I had already died and come back twice and this was the last chance to do it. I must have fallen asleep because when I came to, I was so disoriented that it was frightening. I bolted out of my room and kept wandering around aimlessly, thinking I had just died and come back. My feet were black, and I thought that was from my body dying. I could barely walk, which I thought was also from my body going stiff when I was dying, that they had tried to resuscitate me, but I seemed to just come back on my own.

I wandered round calling out to my twin flame; I had to reconnect with him telepathically. I was asking one of the nurses where he was; I was panicking, I felt that detached. I kept calling out my twin flame's name, wandering round the hospital, asking where he was; there was no reply. Then after what seemed about ten minutes, he said, "I am here." I felt him there with me, and it was such a relief. We had gone together and in the chaos of it all found each other again. I was told telepathically that millions of others had done the same, and that the hospital was expecting it and that hundreds of people would need care because of the trauma of it all. This had to be done to preserve humanity, and the emergency counselling services were on hand to deal with it. The nurses just kept ignoring me or saying very little. One nurse said she knew my partner but she didn't know where he was. My twin flame said that he had been at this hospital once and she had fallen for him; she knew who he was but was so angry from his rejection that she turned sour and evil. I found also that people were hypnotising each other in the hospital just by making eye contact, and she was one of them.

I was told by my spirit guide that I needed a healing bath, that I could change the water to holy water by putting my hands into the water and saying the words, "Holy water." I did this and submerged myself in the bath for about an hour. I felt myself rising in the water, and every time I said, "Holy water," the water would purify even more, and I would rise higher in the bath.

Chapter 8

During my time in hospital, a lot took place. This was a very scary time for me. I was going through different stages of ascension in hospital. I was having contact with people astrally and spiritually, and everything that took place with me was to help others to heal. I also experienced what felt like evil entities in the ward. The nights were the worst. I kept feeling evil presences and had to go into the bathroom to restore my energy. I was told that the toilets and bathrooms were safe for me; I could access sources of energy by standing against the wall. I had to keep going back in there to restore my energy levels and to keep away from negative and evil presences.

I told the hospital staff that I was pregnant, and they took a test to see if this was true. It came back negative but because I was pregnant through immaculate conception, it wouldn't show up; once I was physically intimate with my twin flame, face to face, then the pregnancy would be real. I kept bleeding during my stay, and that scared me as I thought I was miscarrying. I was told by what I thought was my spirit guide that it was breakthrough bleeding and that I needed a stitch, as I had a weak cervix and was having trouble with the entrance to my womb. Apparently, I could have medical treatment spiritually, and this was carried out by a spiritual doctor.

One afternoon, with the presence of various spirits, the procedure was carried out in my room. I felt it was happening, and it certainly felt real; I actually felt as if a stitch was being put in. I was also told by spirits that the bleeding occurred to help others to heal who have had miscarriages. This was achieved by being in my body through astral travel and going through it again in order to heal.

I had a lot of contact with the baby during my time in the hospital. He was a real character, and while I was speaking with various celebrities and famous people telepathically and astrally, he would go to them on the astral plane and speak to them. He had a lot of abilities, such as taking people's abilities away and fighting the dark side.

At one stage while in hospital, I went through a major event. The alarms went off and I was told that there was going to be a major invasion by aliens; the entire world was aware of me, and I had to stop the invasion with my abilities and healing powers. I succeeded in doing this by putting a protective shield around the earth. The American president and the royal family picked up on this and branded me a hero; at that point, I was the messiah and saved the world from evil. I was going to become famous and everyone had tuned in telepathically. At one point, I was in one of the toilets, speaking to millions around the world; people had gathered in various squares around the world to hear me speak telepathically. We were singing and cheering and celebrating this victory.

The next thing that needed to take place was to get me out of hospital. I had tried to get out, but the staff had restrained me. Apparently everyone was tuned in telepathically, including the queen, and was listening to the way I was being treated on the ward. They were appalled and said that I shouldn't be in there, that there was nothing wrong with me, that the staff in the hospital didn't believe me. Although many in the hospital were tuning in telepathically, they felt I was still a threat because of my abilities and because I worked for the government and had dealings with aliens. They were the bad side and were keeping me in hospital because they believed that I was a threat and not that I had these abilities or that I was the messiah. Some felt it was safer there for me for the time being, because of the severity of things outside (people were torn between celebrating and wanting me dead) and due to my dealings with aliens. The hospital (being the government) would not let me be with my twin flame, and on his side, because he worked for the American government, they would not let us be together, because they didn't want peace, which would occur if we reunited.

Some believed us, but still many who worked for the government were the dark side and didn't want us together because we would stop all evil and conquer them. They were the cause of the evil and negativity and therefore had to stop our reunion. The men in black and those directly working for both the British and American government were linking in telepathically and always causing problems for both me and my twin flame. Also the hospital would not allow my twin flame or the queen or anyone who was trying to get me out anywhere near the hospital because of the chaos it might cause. They felt that there would be panic amongst the staff if my twin flame or the queen showed up, due to the instability of many of the patients there.

Then there was the problem of how big this entire situation was, so for that reason I needed to stay put, as I would possibly be hounded by others who felt that I was not the messiah but a cult member. Those that were very religious were furious that I was using the name in vain by saying who I was, and they wanted to hurt me. Many people outside couldn't handle what was happening, and many didn't believe that my twin flame and I were the messiah. So although some were trying to protect me, others were holding me there because of who I said I was. There was such a mix of reactions from people. Some felt because I was saying that I was the messiah that I had to be held there for my own safety, because they believed me and I was such a big figure it wasn't safe to go outside the complex. Some of the public did feel I was the messiah and wanted to meet me to heal and worship me; however, others (the government) just wanted to stop me from succeeding. There was chaos, and many felt that I was a threat rather than a saviour.

Hundreds of celebrities were coming through astrally to meet me and had gone through the ascension process with me but couldn't handle coming back to earth, as it was so traumatic from what had happened. There was such chaos and fear on earth, it was better staying on the astral plane rather than the earth plane until things settled down. The astral plane was full of parties and well-being, and for many back on earth, what was going on was awful. People had been traumatised by what happened. People were trying to get away from the negativity and death that had occurred; many died and didn't want to come back. Every time things got too negative, the world had to move dimensions, and this was very traumatic for people.

I certainly had to steer clear of negativity, as I would die if things got too bad. We had to be one step ahead of the evil and negativity at all times. Moving dimensions was horrendous for me, because I kept feeling as if I was too far away from my twin flame. What happened was weird too, as everything felt out of balance. Our soul went first, and then over time we connected with our bodies. Until our soul connected fully with our bodies, we felt very strange, a kind of feeling of detachment to your body. You felt lost and out of keel. It took time for me and my twin flame to reconnect as well, and when we were not connected, I felt so lost and scared. At one stage, we had moved about eighty levels—the biggest shift ever—and it was very unsettling.

This went on for weeks, moving dimensions and dealing with the shift which was very unsettling. I wandered the halls sprinkling holy water, trying to get rid of the negativity and evil. Sometimes I would come out of my room and be on one dimension and go back in my room and come out again on another dimension. The whole time, the world was listening in telepathically and trying to help me to remove the negativity astrally.

At one stage, I was speaking with many people telepathically, trying to heal them and make the energy positive again. Many different people came through from my past; they were trying to cause problems. Some were spirits of people who had died but were haunting me. Each time, I managed to make peace with them and heal them, thus making the energy positive again. When it was negative, it was draining me, and I had to go into one of the bathrooms to find the positive energy and restore my energy levels.

By the end of the ordeal, I had managed to bring the evil side in and even spoke to the dark side (just like *Star Wars*). They came through and said that they wanted to unite with the light and bring peace to the world.

We all had to work together, and the aliens were even there trying to learn from us about love and peace. They lived off of negativity but wanted to learn how to live with love and live peacefully. I spoke to a tiny species who said that they were trying to learn how to live with love and peace; because there were so many of them, it would take time, as some were still not happy to do so. We had made a breakthrough though and again worked at bringing peace and love to the world. Everyone wanted to find the positive side of things: the press, the government, and the aliens. They knew that the negative side had been winning for so long, and they all wanted to change to bring peace to the world. It was a great feeling at last, that we were all working together now to rid the world of evil and negativity. It would take time, but we would succeed if we all kept staying positive and helping others to change their ways.

Chapter 9

I still was not with my twin flame; we were still apart, and the main culprit at this point was the government. They still did not want us together because then we would win. However, more and more people with the government (the men in black) were on our side and were now protecting me telepathically and through astral travel to keep evil away. At one stage, I had many men in black protecting me, guarding me, and speaking with others in their departments to change and become positive. The main goal was to get me and my twin flame to reunite.

I spent many days and nights speaking with the royal family, spirits, and celebrities, trying to help them to become positive, and they were working on releasing me from hospital.

I fought many a time with the hospital about taking medication, because I was worried that it would harm the baby, and I didn't feel that I needed to take medication, that I could and should do it naturally. They disagreed and insisted time and time again that I take my medication; they didn't believe any of what I was saying about who my partner was or who I was. I spent many days trying to change how things worked in the hospital, to try to get them to be more healing and positive in their steps to helping other patients in the hospital. I told them we can help the other patients by listening to them and healing them naturally through the hands and the heart. They just wouldn't listen, and now the main thing was to get me out of the hospital once and for all. The queen tried, the Prince of Wales tried, but no one at the hospital would take their calls or listen to me. Therefore, the only way was to work telepathically with them and change their ways by communicating by this means. It was working too; more staff were listening telepathically, and they were all trying to get me out of hospital.

I noticed over time that the ambience in the hospital changed and things became more positive. People were playing music and laughing, and the general atmosphere was more bearable. The problem though was that I needed to get out. The queen felt at one stage that in order to get me out, they would have to attempt my release the same way I was brought in: via the police. They would send the KGB in and set the alarms off and rescue me by breaking in while the alarms were going off. In the end, though, they felt this was too high a risk and would be more disturbing than beneficial. Everyone was trying to get me out, but the hospital was not going to allow it to happen. No one's plans were going to work. I was stuck there, and no one could get in or out. I spent days and nights speaking astrally and telepathically with celebrities; it was felt that because my twin flame was a celebrity, this is where my work as a healer would lie. My job would be to help celebrities to get back on their spiritual path by counselling and healing them.

The main problem I still had was with the government in America and in the UK; they would not let me and my twin flame be together. There were many who were interfering and causing problems telepathically. They had caused a lot of what had happened over the weeks by making me experience very traumatic things, hoping that I would be so ruined by what had happened, I would never succeed in winning over the evil. Now, however, they were trying to reverse that, erasing my memory of what had happened and trying to put things right.

It had been discussed in the hospital that I appeal my case for being sectioned, and I decided that I would. Everyone was rooting for me telepathically and would be around astrally to help me win my case. I had my appeal, but they would not approve my release. The hospital still felt that I should be sectioned. This devastated me and all those who were around me. Those outside were running out of options, and if the hospital continued to believe that all I was saying was an illness, I would never get out. I still kept saying that there was nothing wrong with me; I couldn't understand why they didn't believe that I was the messiah and that I needed to be reunited with my twin. That was all I was asking for, but they would not believe me. So I was told I would be staying in hospital. I was devastated; I fought and pleaded with them, to no avail.

It was wonderful being surrounded by celebrities and spirits. We laughed and danced and talked about life morning, noon, and night. I do not think that I slept very much, as I was terrified at night due to hundreds of people astral travelling to me to touch my healing body. There wasn't much that the celebrities in astral travel could do, or the spirits. The only people who seemed to be able to help were the government in astral travel. They would sit outside my room and also come in and tell all these people astral travelling into my room to go. It worked; they all left.

Over time, I managed to get the aliens to move towards the positive side; it wasn't easy, but they were working hard to change.

One ordeal during those months that I will never forget was having to keep my family safe. At one stage, I was told that they were all bad angels, as were all my ex-boyfriends. The only fate for all of them was death. This was horrible, but it was felt that the only way to rid the evil was to send them to their death, unless they changed their ways. The energy from them was so negative and draining, and time and time again we would send them to their death, and they would decide at the last minute that they would change. I did not want to lose my entire family, and I pleaded with them to change. They did try, but at one stage it was felt they couldn't and I would lose my entire family. I was devastated, and the thought of not having my family alive with me was horrendous. All the celebrities that were around me told me that they would look after me and that my twin flame and I would be so wealthy, we would find a way to live out our days peacefully. I couldn't bear it though and pleaded with everyone and my family to not make this fate the inevitable. There was no choice, though; my family were all going to go away and meet their end peacefully. I couldn't bear it; it wasn't fair. I had to accept it though, as we had to think of the earth and wherever there was negative or evil, we had to rid the earth of it. I had to fulfil my duty and role to humanity, and I accepted this fate, not willingly though.

My friends and family came to visit it me in hospital many times. It was hard for me to get them to see what I was saying and experiencing as real. I had spirits around me when my parents were visiting me, but I think they just felt I was still crazy. I had the spirits of Dudley Moore, Peter Cook, and Princess Diana around me (or so I thought). I had the spirits of other celebrities around me at times too, like Jim Morrison. I was speaking to celebrities. I was speaking to the royal family too. At the time I thought this was all real. They were around me astrally and telepathically. People I was talking to telepathically helped me through this ordeal, that is for sure. How did this affect me spiritually? Well, I felt the spirits of Jesus and Mary, so it was definitely a plus in my spiritual beliefs. I felt it was all real, but I look back now and think that the spirits of the dead celebrities must have wondered what I was doing. I laugh to myself now, but I also feel low thinking about how vivid my thoughts were and how I was able to believe that a celebrity was my partner.

Chapter 10

About a week after I was finally released from hospital (the doctors said I was fit enough to leave), I was sitting on the bed at home, channelling Mary. I started to feel that everything that had happened had been all in my head, a lie and just part of my illness. I knew that I had had a nervous breakdown, but I still believed that I was my twin flame's partner and that one day soon, we would be together. I believed that we were closer to meeting, but that we just had to get the government to let us meet. They were trying to get us together, but there were just so many in the government who were still an obstacle. Even after I had come home, I was still convinced that all of this was real, that I was going to be rich, and that it was the government that was stopping me and my twin flame from reuniting. My twin flame was having to decide at this point whether to stay in the UK at a undisclosed location or go home to the United States. He could go home and we could speak on the phone and make it real.

Then one evening, I was in my room and just started questioning the events that had taken place, as my twin flame started to talk about a lot of things that were not true (e.g., that he had received a large sum of money which we would be splitting and that I would be a celebrity and very well off). None of it made sense, and the more we talked telepathically, the more I was finding out that so much that had been said had been twisted and blown out of proportion. What was true then; how much of it was real?

Then suddenly, I just fell apart. I just realised that my twin flame had never been talking to me, that I wasn't rich and famous, and that the past three months had been a result of my illness. I was devastated and lost. I couldn't believe what had happened. I hadn't channelled all these spirits or spoken to these celebrities astrally or telepathically. I had been ill, very ill, and now it had hit home; I had suffered a psychotic breakdown and I was lucky to still have my job (I hadn't resigned). After all that I had done, I had been through hell and lost what I felt was everything in my life.

I never had a partner; I never had these abilities, healing powers, or connections with celebrities; I was ill. This was the beginning of the downhill spiral of anxiety, loss, confusion, and sadness. I was depressed, lost, and feeling like I had nothing left in my life. I had fallen in love with a man who had never been around. I never had a twin flame, I never had a baby, I never saved the world, and I had never had true love. I was now sitting in my room speechless. I was disoriented and left with an emptiness I cannot describe. I could not imagine what my friends must think of me after everything I had done, said, and gone through. I had done it all on my own. I had never had the support network that I felt was there; it was just a figment of my imagination. Can the brain do all this? Can my mind make such a world of lies and beliefs? How could this be? It was not fair; it was cruel and devastating.

I wondered how my breakdown had affected my friends. They had seen what I was going through, what I was saying and doing. What did they think of it all?

I know that this experience left me lost spiritually. I didn't believe in the spirit world anymore, I didn't believe in spirit guides or life after death. I thought, how can it be real when it wasn't real for three months? How can this be possible? What is real for me? I thought

I had channelled spirits, but in fact it had been my illness. I know I can speak to the spirit world, and I have in the past, but from September to November, so much of it was lies and unreal that I didn't know what to believe anymore.

Chapter 11

To this day, the whole experience has left me wondering what to believe about spirituality. It left me with doubt and so many questions about whether I can talk to spirits. I wonder if they are around me and how I can tell the difference between what is real and what is not real. I was back on the fence. For months, I was viewing this subject as complete rubbish. I didn't believe in any of it. Not in aliens, not in angels, and definitely not in spirits. I was devastated! I had found happiness learning and discovering life after death, and now I had to convince myself that the spirit world was real. I couldn't; I couldn't sense spirit, I couldn't sense my spirit guides, and I couldn't see into the future like before. I was lost, miserable, and depressed. The once newfound joy was now utter desperation.

However, slowly over time, I told myself that I had to rediscover this path of mine. I had to find out the truth and search for answers once again. I needed to get back in touch with my spiritual beliefs and find that happiness and peace that had overwhelmed me a year ago. How? How could I get my abilities back? They were gone and I was so miserable it was untrue. I was angry and a sceptic again.

The only thing I could do was start listening to radio podcasts again, listen, absorb, and start to relearn and rediscover what I had learnt and discovered before. This helped, and over time, I started to understand and believe that there was something out there we couldn't see or hear. I was starting to retrace my steps spiritually and find the meaning of what life is all about again. It took months, but revisiting these areas was enabling me to find the truth once again.

I started going on ghost hunts again and using my abilities to channel spirits. I was starting to sense the presence of spirit, and this excited me. I was getting back my beliefs and abilities. From when I left hospital, it took me about eight months to get back on my spiritual path. I didn't feel I was there yet completely, but a lot of what I believed before (e.g., energies, reiki, the spirit world, aliens) I am starting to believe is real or at least possible. I am still trying to understand it all, but I certainly feel I have gotten a lot closer to where I want to be. I am still struggling with sensing things and understanding them, but I feel with a lot of reading and time, I will get back where I was a year ago. I know I am stronger and more at peace than I ever was before.

Chapter 12

As I am writing this in July 2009, I am having to come to terms with another admission to hospital. I was in hospital for six months. It all started when I was in the lounge of the house I was living in and my spirit guide came through and said that my twin flame wanted to speak to me telepathically. I was floored, as I had just gotten over him and cut him out of the picture. How could he then pop up again in my life? That is when things went downhill. I got carted away to the hospital in January for having hallucinations and delusional beliefs again, not eating, not sleeping, and isolating myself. I have just gone through the same scenario as 2007, a so-called psychotic episode (i.e., seeing things and feeling like I am talking telepathically to famous people and my twin).

This time, I saw a lot of things in the house that I was in. I saw a lot in the hospital too. I saw people in period costume and beings with small bodies and massive heads (like a Mr. Potato Head); I saw children in the bushes under the window of my room, and I saw children down the corridor. In the house I saw faeries and creatures from *Star Wars*; heard the voice of Darth Vader; and saw Chewbacca, gremlins, massive butterflies, and endangered or extinct animals on the walls like I was being shown a short film. I saw this huge mass in the shape of a worm coming out of the wall. It was the same scenario where if this guy and I reunite, we will help bring world peace. That the dark side and evil are battling with the light, and I was talking to leaders in all areas telepathically (e.g., the Illuminati, Freemasons, the Mafia, the CIA, Secret Service, aliens) to stop controlling the world with negativity and fear. To work towards peace throughout the world and the universe, and I was leading the way. That my twin flame and I are a threat and those in high places both on earth and in the spirit world were trying to interfere; I thought that people in the house were evil and trying to take my life, but I screamed, "I don't want to die!" I also asked my twin flame to help me. He came through and the light reversed what was happening. I was told that is what it feels like when you die before it is your time.

While in hospital I was given an injection twice, and I was told telepathically it was lethal, but because of who I was, it wouldn't kill me. I don't know what is real and what is just in my head. I basically was going through the same scenario this time as last time, thinking that I was pregnant through astral sex and that my twin flame and I were going to be very rich and famous, and if we reunited, there would be world peace. I was talking to friends and family telepathically, and everyone was astral travelling to me. Those in power were putting fear into my mind with unpleasant thoughts and images through mind manipulation and mind control (e.g., bad dreams, horrific images such as dead bodies, being stabbed, or injected with lethal drugs to get rid of me).

Chapter 13

I sit in the house feeling devastated again that most of what I went through was not real, that I am not pregnant, that there is no sign of all this being a dream come true. The major scenario in hospital was that everyone united after about four months of battling evil and the dark side. I battled with those telepathically who didn't want peace but wanted a new world order, where there was going to be a mass suicide and total control (i.e., people walking the streets would not be able to make noise while walking about their daily lives). It was my job to convince those in power to work towards world peace.

My final thoughts on things again are what is real and what is not? Why did I go through the same scenario again? I spoke with a few patients while I was in hospital, and they were complaining of the same thing, seeing and hearing things all with the same diagnosis: psychosis. So can we see more in a different frame of mind? Was this scenario of mine messages and premonitions of what is going on around us in the real world? I did see in hospital what to me were visions. The first one was baby clothes lined up: pink and blue baby suits. Then down the corridor, I saw lots of balloons, pigeons feeding, and water.

What does it all mean? As I explored what other people are feeling and experiencing, I did see a connection: spiritual awakening at its finest. People I talk to say there is a shift in consciousness and we are becoming more open to things we normally cannot see or hear. The sad thing is that sceptics and those in medicine only see the symptoms. How can we combat mental illness to be linked to the paranormal?

While I was in hospital, I got the chance to be interviewed in front of an audience about my experience and how it could be linked to the paranormal. They didn't give me much feedback, and I know I was unwell, which probably was more what they were thinking, rather than a link with the paranormal. I do believe that in a certain frame of mind, we can see and hear more. I see people all over the Internet saying they were poorly over the last two years (i.e., breakdowns, psychosis, vertigo, and other illnesses) and becoming more open to things. I have also discovered there is a huge increase in interest in spirituality, life after death, telepathic connections, astral travel, and so on. People are rising up who won't stand for any more control, who are questioning everything. They see that those in power need to be stopped because people want to be free to explore and think for themselves to live life with peace and love around them. We must stop the spread of fear and control created by those in charge.

I do see a battle going on between dark and light all around us. The light will not stand for any more negativity because that is what we have endured for the last 2,000 years. The dark side is still trying to put fear in our minds, and the light is fighting to bring things out into the open, like 9/11, the assassination of JFK, 2012, and terrorism. The dark want another war and the light want world peace. People are retaliating and speaking out, as there is too much negativity around. I was told by spirit that a certain leader was the second coming, and while I was in hospital, I thought I was talking to him telepathically and we were fighting together to stop the dark side from winning.

So as I struggle with having been diagnosed with a mental illness and coming to terms with things, the world is at war. Well, isn't that what I was experiencing while I was in hospital both times?

Chapter 14

In November 2010, I felt like I was relapsing again. I started having the same symptoms: my thoughts were racing, and I was hearing things. One morning, I woke up at the crack of dawn and saw something flying past my window; it was shaped like Battlestar Galactica. Then I saw a battle breaking out in the sky. White lasers were shooting back and forth in the sky, through the clouds, hundreds of them. It seemed to go on for days. I saw a plume of smoke at the back of the house across the street. It looked like the lasers from *Star Wars*, but white ones instead of red ones. I saw what I thought were Paladeans, extraterrestrial beings, being taken out of the house across the street. They were taken out of the house and put into a van; people I thought were Jedis in uniform laid them on a large flat object and blew them up. I was told by my spirit guide that there were Paladeans in the houses two and three doors down and in the house across the street (these are the houses I had the confrontations with between January and March 2011).

That is all I can remember from that morning. Over the next few weeks, I saw people in the back of a truck in either astral travel or spirit. I saw Mother Nature in the back garden of the house three doors down. I saw Jack Frost in my window, and I saw people hanging from the tree across the street from me; I didn't know why that was happening. The scene kept on changing from a nice scene to a horrible scene. I saw big toys and dragons in the sky, and I also saw dinosaurs. I saw a pterodactyl in the sky about a week later.

I was astral travelling through dimensions again, and Dudley Moore was there. I kept talking to my figurines on the shelf, and Buzz Lightyear was chasing Dudley Moore; I saw red lasers coming out of his guns as Dudley ran away. Dudley and I had to keep changing dimensions again and find a safe dimension, as most of the dimensions were not nice at all, and I felt we shouldn't be there. There was a strange sort of lighting on the dimensions where we shouldn't be, and I thought that if we stayed, the Illuminati would catch up with us. They were all in black robes. The energy was calm and peaceful in the safer dimensions. Where we were not supposed to be, the energy was awful and I felt scared. I felt we had to hurry and move dimensions to keep one step ahead of the Illuminati.

I saw people inside the mirror of my wardrobe, watching me and spying on me with camcorders and cameras. I was told they were Paladeans and they wanted to observe what I was doing, but I didn't know why. There was a reception area in the mirror with people milling about and walking past the reception and standing around. Then the scene in my mirror changed into a shop with baskets of vegetables and a crib with a cover over it. I didn't know why this happened; I felt it was a message from whoever was in the wardrobe, telling me they wanted to make peace and wanted to change.

Then Peter Cook joined me and Dudley Moore, and we were making audiotapes and I was interviewed by Peter Cook for a week. I did disappear for about three days in astral travel, and they were both freaking out. I was trying to find out where they were because I wasn't sure if they were in the other room, in the loft, or inside my bed. We were making lots of tapes, talking about what I was going through and day-by-day events.

In December, I was talking to a lot of people in spirit which is when I saw Jack Frost in my window; it was around Christmas time. I also saw Santa Claus in the sky; he looked like someone pulling a sleigh. I bought loads of food and decorated my house with a Santa and some flowers and lay in the lounge, watching movies. Although I was alone, I didn't feel alone. Judy Garland was around, so were Peter Cook, Dudley Moore, and Princess Diana. I had lots of food and enjoyed Christmas on my own with friends in spirit. I never felt alone; that was the nice thing. Now looking back, this is when I realised that being a medium was my true path. Being able to speak to so many people in spirit was a wonderful thing, plus what I saw in the sky and around the neighbourhood (e.g., Jack Frost and Mother Nature).

I went down to London for a few days and felt I was speaking to Buddha, who said to only go down for two days. I booked my ticket and headed down to London all by myself. The night I got there, which was December 28, was a horrible night for me. The first hotel I went to had dozens of North Americans there; I thought they were all there for a mass suicide. I checked into my room; it had awful décor and the layout freaked me out, so did the hotel. My floor had long narrow corridors, and each door was the same; it was very claustrophobic and had a terrible feel to it. The room was even worse. I was scared that I was going to be gassed in there and never get out alive, so I left in a hurry. I managed to find another hotel via the help of Princess Diana, as she was there with me.

Boy, what a night it was. I checked into the other hotel room and then ordered room service. I went for a walk and ended up at Hyde Park, where there was a Christmas Fayre going on. Walking through the Fayre was amazing but at the same time overwhelming. The Christmas Fayre was huge and went on forever. I ended staying for quite a while, just wandering round and taking in the views. There was an ice rink, swings for the kids, a circus, a ride playing the Paramount song, and also a ride playing the theme song from *Star Wars* which overwhelmed me. I could go on forever about what was there. I went into the circus and noticed that there were no animals there, just a woman showing the audience various strength movements to the song from *Gladiator* (which happened to be my favourite song on the album). I started crying when I heard the song, because I thought this fayre was a message to me about world peace; I thought this Christmas Fayre was a sign that it was happening. As you enter Hyde Park, there are lights all around, and it is really hard to describe how wonderful the décor was. I thought this was a message from the Paladeans and Venusians that world peace was on our doorstep.

I also went to Buckingham Palace and noticed that all the lights were down; I was told telepathically that the queen was trying to show her appreciation for all that I had done the last four years with world peace. The guards' heads were down, and the queen had told them to do that, as she knew I was visiting London. I asked one of the guards if the queen was in, but he said she wasn't at home. Looking back, this was so humiliating for me, as I was still in the same outfit I had worn when I arrived with my suitcase. I went back to Hyde Park which had no lights on except for old Victorian lamps; they made the park look lovely. All of this I thought was for me from the queen to show her appreciation for all that I had done. A lot of people were with me in astral travel and in spirit, including Ofra Haza and Princess Diana. I went back to the hotel and then left to go to a spa but got disoriented and ended up walking around London for six hours with people with me in astral travel and in spirit.

I ended up walking over to Big Ben; Dudley Moore was with me, and we went to phone boxes and messed around, pretending to ring each other. I was trying to find him by ringing the number on the phone box. I then went back to Big Ben and was told telepathically to listen for the chime at eleven o'clock. I did and everyone was listening telepathically. I leaned against the iron gates when Big Ben chimed at eleven o'clock; it was a wonderful moment.

I went back to the hotel and stayed up for most of the night talking to people telepathically, listening to music and smoking in the hotel room. I had a wonderful time until the next morning, when the hotel asked me to leave. I wanted to stay in London a week and go to London Zoo and see the animals, especially Zaire the gorilla. Now I had to find somewhere else to stay. I had tried Saturday evening to get clothes but became disoriented and wandered around London for six hours with people in spirit and astral travel. So I was stuck with the same outfit I arrived in, muddy jeans which were soaking wet and the same top and jacket. I left the hotel and tried to find another hotel to stay in, as everyone I was talking to telepathically wanted me to stay in London for another few days at least. I could barely walk after having walked for six hours the day before. I was wearing the same shoes and outfit, wandering around London trying to book myself into another hotel. People were there in astral travel helping me walk to another hotel. We all decided it was better to go to Regent's Park and book myself into a hotel there, as I didn't have any luck finding a hotel around Hyde Park.

I went to the Green Park tube station, but when I tried to get money out, I found my bank account had been frozen. Now I thought I was stranded and my train ticket was out of date. Queen Elizabeth I was with me and said she would get me home. I didn't want to go but everyone said it was best to get back on the train to Leeds. By this time, Judy Garland, Queen Elizabeth I, Peter Cook, and Dudley Moore were with me. I soon realised my train ticket was an open first-class ticket, and I was able to get all the way back to Kings Cross station and get on the train back to Leeds; it felt right to do so as well. While I was on the train, I realised that what Buddha had predicted matched the dates: two days. I arrived in London on December 28 and the day I returned to Leeds was December 30, 2010. Amazing!

This journey left me exhausted and humiliated, as my clothes were not, shall we say, in good condition by the time I left London, but by the time I got back to Leeds, it felt right, and everyone was saying telepathically how awful London was and how wonderful it would be to live in Yorkshire. Homeward bound I went.

Chapter 15

In December 2010 and February 2011, I kept seeing a lot of strange things in the sky. In December, I saw three round balls with tails in the sky. One of them was large and two were medium sized; they all moved horizontally to each other. In February, I saw the same but not as big in the sky and more of them all moving horizontal to each other. I didn't know what they were.

Four years ago, I wanted to walk away from being a medium, but after being ill again in November 2010, I knew I couldn't. I loved Christmastime and being with spirit, eating lots of lovely food, and having spirit helping me. I still feel them around me from time to time, especially Dudley Moore and Ofra Haza (when I play her music). I know this journey the past four years has changed me a lot, and I am excited to share this book with you as I have seen so much, a lot of which I feel is paranormal. I have also met a lot of people over the last six months who have helped me piece things together. I am still not sure what to make of all this, other than yes, I wasn't well, but also how you can see more in a certain frame of mind. Last but not least, I am a medium, so was I talking to spirit? Yes, most of the time I believe I was, as I am a medium, so it does makes sense. I have had my questions answered, for I went to a spiritual fair in March and read that you see hallucinations through your third eye. That is where mediums see spirit and have visions—through the third eye. So what did I see? Can I see more as a medium compared to others?

About the Author

※

Christy is a Medium who has been living in the UK for 16 years. She has travelled all over Yorkshire doing Paranormal Investigations. She emigrated to London, England from Toronto, Canada in 1996. She currently lives with her Cat Daisy in Leeds, West Yorkshire.

Printed in Great Britain
by Amazon